GETTING IT TOGETHER

GETTING IT

TOGETHER

THE BLACK MAN'S GUIDE
TO GOOD GROOMING AND FASHION

by Mike Fields

with contributions by A. Peter Bailey
photographs by Bert Andrews
drawings by Kenneth Hunter

DODD, MEAD & COMPANY   NEW YORK

PUBLISHED BY DODD, MEAD & COMPANY, INC.
79 MADISON AVENUE, NEW YORK, N.Y., 10016
DISTRIBUTED IN CANADA BY
MCCLELLAND AND STEWART LIMITED, TORONTO
MANUFACTURED IN THE UNITED STATES OF AMERICA
DESIGNED BY JUDITH LERNER
SECOND PRINTING   HL384

LIBRARY OF CONGRESS CATALOGING IN PUBLICATION DATA

FIELDS, MIKE.
   GETTING IT TOGETHER.

   INCLUDES INDEX.
   1. GROOMING FOR MEN.   2. AFRO-AMERICAN MEN—HEALTH
AND HYGIENE.   3. MEN'S CLOTHING.   4. AFRO-AMERICANS—
CLOTHING.   I. BAILEY, A. PETER.   II. TITLE.
RA777.8.F53 1983   646.7'088041   83-8919
ISBN 0-396-08177-0 (pbk.)

THIS BOOK IS DEDICATED TO MY FAMILY

ESPECIALLY MY WONDERFUL GREAT-NEPHEWS

Alfred Fields, A-Arkieam R. Fields, and DeShane Granger

*

AND TO MY DEAR DECEASED FRIEND

Emmett Andrews,

WHO SPENT MANY HOURS IN THE DARKROOM PRINTING ALL THE PHOTOS.

HE WOULD BE PROUD OF THE FINISHED PRODUCT.

Contents

Acknowledgments

THIS IS MY FIRST BOOK, so there are many people I have to thank. Without them, this book and acquiring the knowledge to write it would not have been possible.

First, my agent, Roslyn Targ, for believing in me and the book. Jerry Ford, for his help and for selecting me to be the first black male model to sign with his agency. Evan Marshall, my editor, who got things going in the right direction. Many thanks to the people who so generously gave their assistance: Dr. John Harris, podiatrist; hair specialists Stanley James, Black Rose, Finney, Harold Melvin, Joseph Mosely, and James Cain. Thanks to Dr. George R. Jordan and Dr. Melvin Alexander, prominent dermatologists, and Ms. Arlene Hawkins, well-known beauty consultant, who provided valuable information on skin care for black men. Nathan Busch, a prominent hair and skin specialist, was a great asset. Many thanks to Richard V. Clarke, Gil Gainey, Debbie Reese, and Angela Smith. Their information and research was vital to this book.

My hat is off to Arthur McGee, Andrew Pollack, Gene Edey, Pierre Cardin, Barbara Kotlikoff, PONY, Gentleman's Quarters, Coats Plus, Gatner swimwear, A. J. Lester, and Sasson swimwear. Without them nearly everyone would be nude. So thanks for the beautiful clothes.

For nearly fifteen years I have been producing male fashion shows, the backbone of my learning experience. There are some people I have to thank, not only for their participation, but also for their encouragement, inspiration, and just always being there when I needed them.

Dionne Warwick, my friend, who never let me down and told me to hang in there: you know I love you. Gladys Knight, Bubba Knight, Edward Patten, and William Guest—my other family—for putting their stage image in my hands and for being my friends for twenty years: here it is finally. Thank you, Patti LaBelle, Sarah Dash, and Nona Hendryx, for all those fashion shows, all that love, encouragement, and friendship. Freda Payne, you are beautiful. And thanks for all your help, Tommy Jonsen, Arlene Rolant, and Sandra McPhearson. Ditto to The Temptations' Melvin Franklin, Otis Wilson, and Dennis Edwards.

I have to thank George Branford and Ophelia DeVore for starting me in modeling. Thanks, Burgess Owens, for the fashion shows and for appearing in the book; you are the greatest. You, too, Gerry Bledsoe; you never let me down. Thanks to you, too, Frankie Crocker. Ditto to Bobby Hunter, Jimmy Randolph, Chuck Jackson (my friend, who always answers when I call), Jim Tyrrell, Win Wilford, G. Keith Alexander, and Vaughn Harper. Rita Griffin, what can I say? It would be easier to move Detroit next to New York. Thanks for all the traveling and love. Susan Taylor, you said I could do it, so here it is. Charles Sanders, your advice was invaluable and our friendship deepened. Thanks for letting me worry you this long. O.K., Angie Aqular, this is for you: "I need something typed right away," love, Mike. Peter Long, Loretta Long, thanks for all those years of help, for your teaching, your encouragement, and mostly your love; I could not have done it without you. Yvonne Fair and Sammy Strain, you have always been in my corner; I hope you are as pleased as I am. Walter Godfrey, my running buddy and biggest fan. Everything came up smelling like a rose. Thanks for providing a shoulder to lean on.

Lastly, I am forever grateful to the models for their time and effort. Without them I would have been in serious trouble. And to Bert Andrews, who gave his all so that the photos would come out right, which they did, and I will love him forever because of it. A. Peter Bailey and Kenneth Hunter, we did it. Thanks.

Foreword

AS AN AWARE and very fashion-conscious person, I am quite relieved to know that someone with Mike Fields' expertise and credentials in the world of fashion has taken the time to make our black men aware of the wonderful ways to look and be looked at.

With the combined efforts of people in the fashion industry and Michael guiding this project, I know without a doubt that it will be successful. *Getting It Together* is much needed, and finally it's here.

DIONNE WARWICK

Introduction

THIS BOOK is important for two main reasons. Not only is it the first book to focus on the grooming and fashion problems of the black man, but it also shows clearly that these problems cannot be dismissed with a brief mention, as white-oriented books and magazines on grooming and fashion are wont to do.

The black man's grooming and fashion problems are unique. For example, he must give special attention to conditioning and styling his hair, to shaving, and to selecting and accessorizing an outfit according to his particular color tone. This book addresses these problems and many more.

The black man has a style all his own, adding a certain flair to design and colors. Rarely can others dictate his taste; he knows what he likes. Black men are the heaviest consumers, per capita, of men's apparel, with yearly expenditures estimated to be in the billions of dollars. Nowhere is the clothing industry's recognition of this fact more apparent than in the leading general-readership magazines, newspapers, and trade journals, where it is no longer surprising to find black models wearing the latest designer fashions. This book also addresses itself to fashion for the black man, including the basic principles of good dress for the black brothers who are just beginning to "get it together."

Since the beginning of my modeling career in 1960, I have been convinced that black men—especially young black men—needed a basic grooming and fashion guide to help them develop self-expression, self-confidence, poise, dignity, and above all, a sense of self. That's no less than the black man deserves, and I'm delighted to offer that guide now. I hope *Getting It Together* answers all your questions.

MIKE FIELDS

Grooming

1
HAIR

ALL TOO OFTEN, black men have thought of their hair as a source of problems. It had dandruff. It was hard to comb. It got dirty too easily. It fell out too soon. And for years, in an effort to deal with these problems, many men opted for the easy but not always effective way out—going to the barber every two weeks and getting their hair cut just this side of bald. In some circles this was known as "getting it cut down to the good hair." Then all you had to do was put on a little pomade or Royal Crown gel, slip on a stocking cap overnight, and—presto!—you had waves rather than kinks. For those who resisted the short cut, a "solution" was to have their hair "processed," or "conked"—the black man's way of saying that, like most black women, he was having his hair straightened.

The heavy emphasis on Black Pride in the 1960s changed all this. Most black men began to wear their hair in a natural style, throwing away the stocking caps and processing equipment and glorying in their kinks and curls. Unfortunately, some went so far as to believe that wearing their hair natural meant that they didn't have to wash or comb it; as a result, their hair often resembled a bird's nest. But most black men were very conscious of

3

their hair's appearance, and attractive "fros" of various lengths began popping up all over the country.

In the beginning, the style was not only an aesthetic change but also a political statement. In the schools, in the military service, in the corporate world, in the sports world, and often in men's own homes, opposition to the new style could be strong and sharp. The style soon spread abroad, where it took on an even greater political significance. During a 1974 visit to Brazil, a country whose government is extremely wary of any sign of Black Consciousness among its black citizens, I was told that if a black man wore a "fro," he was considered persona non grata by government and private employers.

Finally, in the early 1970s, the new hair style became acceptable. By that time most barbers and hair stylists, while not exactly crazy about the style (since it meant that men were getting haircuts every six to eight weeks rather than every two), had adjusted their prices and accepted it. So had most of the other opposition forces. Today the "fro" remains popular with many but in a more restricted form. Others have gone back to short hair, stocking caps, and waves, while still others have turned to a somewhat more sophisticated version of the old straightening process. This is referred to as "relaxing" the hair, an effect brought about by products containing sodium hydroxide (lye), calcium hydroxide, and ammonium thioglycolate. The first two make kinky hair straight, while the last is used to create the curly permanent known as jherrie curls.

The most important point to remember is that whatever the style, basic hair-care needs remain constant, and you must be aware of them if your hair is to stay healthy and look its best.

For advice on care of the hair and scalp, we went to six acknowledged experts, each a specialist with at least fifteen years of experience in taking care of black hair.

Black Rose (Nehlms), a former chemist and quality-control expert at Revlon, was a pioneer in the wearing, cutting, and treatment of the natural hair style; he now works out of the Casdulan Salon, in Harlem. James Finney, known professionally simply as Finney, has a shop on Manhattan's West Side and is nationally known for his plaiting style. Stanley James, a hair stylist, grooming consultant, and makeup artist, works out of the Donald Scott Salon on Manhattan's East Side. Harold Melvin, the first black hairdresser to work on feature films and receive full screen credits, now has a salon on Manhattan's West Side. Joseph Mosely, an innovator in hair and skin research that has been effectively applied to blacks, owns Dermalax Systems, Inc., of Brooklyn. And James Cain is a barber at the Hair Affair Barber Shop in Harlem.

HAIR BASICS

All hair is composed of nitrogen, sulfur, water, iron traces, and amino acids. Its basic parts are the follicle, a small saclike gland in the body from which the hair grows; the papilla, a small bud at the base of the follicle; the sebaceous gland, which supplies oil to the skin and hair; and the shaft, or hair fiber itself.

Hair is lubricated by sebum oil secreted by the sebaceous glands. The amount of oil secreted by these glands determines the relative dryness or oiliness of the hair. The kinky, tightly curled hair characteristic of most black men tends toward dryness, because the tight curls can cause the natural oils from the sebaceous glands to be unevenly dispersed.

There is absolutely no way to have healthy hair if you don't take care of your body. Your diet should include plenty of nutritious foods, such as fresh vegetables and fruits (see Chapter 3). Also remember that your hair cannot be fed externally by direct application of vitamin shampoos or any other so-called hair foods. For healthy hair you must take your vitamins internally. Your doctor can provide you with a nutrition chart.

Finally you should remember that although your hair can be kinky or straight, curly or tangled, dirty or clean, blond or black, shiny or dull, it can *never* be "bad" or "good." Much too often among black folks, straight hair is described as "good hair" and kinky hair as "bad hair." This type of self-deprecating usage must be eliminated if we are to take proper, educated care of our hair.

SHAMPOOING

Accept the fact that to shampoo your hair correctly and get the best results, you're going to have to take an extra few minutes. Dabbing on a little shampoo and rinsing it out just won't do it. The extra time you take can mean the difference between a clean and healthy head of hair and a head full of unnecessary problems.

Since black hair tends to be dry, our experts generally recommend an oil-based shampoo, which will help replenish natural oils that are lost in the cleaning process. Some of these shampoos contain coconut oil or have an herbal base; usually the words "For Dry Hair" will be written on the bottle. Never use soap in lieu of shampoo. Soap's high alkaline content is tough on the hair's natural oils.

Before shampooing, the hair should be given a hot oil treatment, which helps to soften dead skin on the scalp. If you are shampooing at home, you can warm up mineral or olive oil and massage it gently into your scalp with your fingertips.

The shampooing itself should be done with massaging as well as cleaning in mind. A vigorous massage with the fingertips, taking care not to bruise or cut the scalp with the fingernails, helps to increase the flow of blood into the scalp area, thus providing more nutrients for the hair.

How often you should shampoo depends on your particular hair needs and your life-style. According to our experts, if the shampooing is done correctly, once a week may be sufficient for the average man. However, if you lead a very active life or work in an environment where your hair is exposed to dirt, you should shampoo more often—at least three times a week, and even more if necessary. Again, the key is to take the extra few minutes to do it correctly. For those who wear plaits, remember that shampooing can be done without removing them. And don't forget to rinse the shampoo thoroughly from your hair. Shampoo left in the hair gives it a dull look and can dry to produce dandruff-like flakes.

After shampooing and before combing, the scalp and hair should be lubricated with a light, nonchemical oil. If you wear a long natural, be sure to lubricate it out to the ends, since the oils produced by the body don't reach the ends of long naturals. It is best, if possible, to put the oil into the hair while it is still wet and to let the hair dry naturally. This allows the oil to thoroughly penetrate the hair and scalp. Be careful not to overuse oils, since an excess can clog scalp pores, attract dirt, and leave you with greasy-looking hair. Also be very careful if you use a blow dryer, since black hair is fragile and breaks easily, and the dryer may rob it of the much-needed moisture you've replaced by oiling.

COMBING OUT

All the shampooing, massaging, and oiling, no matter how correctly done, will be for naught if the next process in hair care is incorrectly done—combing. Our experts generally agree that most men don't know how to comb their hair correctly, a problem that leads to unnecessary and extensive hair breakage. There is a right way to comb your hair, and you must follow it if you want a head of hair that is truly a crown of glory. Like shampooing, it takes a few extra minutes, but the results are well worth it.

The first recommendation is to comb your hair while it is still wet, when it has more elasticity. Since, again, our hair is particularly fragile, whether wet or dry, it should be combed with patience and caution.

The most important thing to remember is that your

comb, or your pik if you wear a long natural, must have widely spaced teeth with blunt ends, which won't pull the hair out or harm the scalp. Several experts recommend combing the hair before picking it. It's also important to note that cleaning and combing the hair correctly is a waste of time and effort if you comb it with a dirty comb or pik.

Bring the comb gently through the hair, front to back. The comb should glide through your hair. This is especially important if you are wearing a long natural, which must be patiently combed all the way out. You should also keep the natural clipped at the ends to help prevent tangling and breakage. If your hair becomes tangled, use your fingertips to gently and patiently pull out the snaps.

Remember that combing your hair every day, no matter how gently, is bound to cause some breakage and hair

loss. That's why some black men who want their hair to grow have it plaited. For some, this has become an alternative to wearing the hair short or in a long natural. The plaits, which can stay in up to three months, need no combing, thus allowing the hair to repair itself and grow. Remember, however, that not needing combing does not mean not needing cleaning and oiling. Both are still vital.

As for brushing for black men, it's okay if your hair is cut very short or is straight, but it's not too effective for black hair worn in a natural or in plaits.

CONDITIONING

If your hair is properly cared for—cleaned and oiled regularly and thoroughly—you may not need to use a conditioner. However, this is a decision that you shouldn't make yourself. You should seek the advice of a qualified hair-care professional, who will tell you what conditioner, if any, is needed.

Mike Fields

Whether or not you need a conditioner is determined not only by the natural oiliness or dryness of your hair, but also by your life-style and the season of the year. For instance, a conditioning is recommended in the spring and fall to help rejuvenate the hair after the dryness of the winter and the humidity of the summer, respectively. Winter is an especially bad time for us, because we usually cover our hair with wool caps for warmth. These caps are notorious for pulling out hair, and it is highly recommended that you wear a scarf or stocking cap under your wool cap to prevent hair loss.

If your hair-care professional advises the use of a conditioner, you should carefully read the instructions and use it correctly. Remember that the conditioner's purpose is to give the hair body and to lubricate individual hair shafts. It helps to restore softness, shine, and manageability. Like shampoos, different conditioners are designed to deal with different hair problems. Pay special attention to how long the conditioner should be left in the hair. Leaving a conditioner in that should be rinsed out can cause severe hair damage.

CHOOSING A STYLE

The structure of your face should determine your choice of a hairstyle. Your hair-care professional can advise you on the most flattering style, but there are principles you should know about the four basic facial structures:

The round face needs the contrast of vertical, angular lines. Let the hair grow a little long; a closely cropped style will accentuate the roundness of your face. If you wear a part, it should be low. For a triangular look—an

the round face

the oval face

the square face

the long and narrow face

effective way of offsetting roundness in the face—wear your hair low on one side and high on the other.

The oval face, like the round, needs contrasting vertical lines. I would suggest that you wear your hair close on the sides and long on top. If possible, pull a little hair down over your forehead to break up this area. Sideburns should be short to medium.

The square face needs roundness in the hairstyle. Wear a part high on the head, with your hair cut low on one side and high on the other. Sideburns should be medium to long.

The long and narrow face needs fullness in the hairstyle. One way of achieving this is to comb the hair straight back and to wear it low on the nape of the neck, which is usually long. If you want to wear a part, angle it a little toward the center of the head, so that it will give some indication of width.

HAIR LOSS AND REPLACEMENT

Every day of your life, you lose some of your hair. Normally, and if you are taking care of your hair properly, this hair is replaced. However, excessive breakage, illness, or neglect may contribute to the permanent loss of some or all of your hair. Your response to this will, of course, depend on your personal needs and desires, involving vanity and perhaps even job considerations. You can elect either to let your head remain bald or to get a hairpiece, weave, or transplantation. Several of our experts resolutely support the bald look—if there are no unsightly lumps or bumps on the head. Some people consider a well-shaped bald head a great turn-on. If you opt for a hairpiece, it is highly recommended that you be very sure of its quality and of its natural look. You will definitely need the help of a professional as you make your choice. Likewise with the weave, which is usually recommended when the hair is thinning. In weaving, your remaining hair is corn-rowed, and the new hair, usually synthetic, is woven into it. At least every six weeks you must go back to the weaver and have it tightened. Otherwise it will become loose and look bad and may actually pull out your remaining hair. Transplantation, another option, is not readily recommended by any of our experts. In this procedure a plug of skin with hair in it, taken from elsewhere on the head, is plugged right into the scalp. As can be imagined, the process can be expensive (depending on how much hair has to be replaced), lengthy, and not guaranteed to last forever. Give all of the replacement procedures careful consideration, and get the advice of a qualified hair-care professional.

THE USE OF CHEMICALS

If you are interested in having your hair relaxed (the current term for straightening) or getting the curly perm known as jherri curls, you must first consider whether the expense and time needed are worth it to you. If you do decide to go ahead, you must have the procedure done by a qualified professional. To relax the hair, he or she will apply the creamy solution with either the back of a comb or the fingers, from the nape of the neck forward in small sections. Once the hair is thoroughly processed, it is rinsed out and then shampooed with a low-pH shampoo to help stabilize the new straightness. The process usually

Mike Fields

takes from two and a half to three hours, and every six to eight weeks the roots should be touched up to maintain the style.

For the curly perm (usually the jherri curls), the hair is first relaxed and rinsed, and then a conditioner is applied. A perm lotion is then applied to the hair, which is rolled on perm rods. After two short periods under the dryer the rods are removed and—presto!—you have curls. The style has to be retouched at the roots every twelve to sixteen weeks, but should last as long as you want it to if it's cared for properly. Both relaxed hair and jherri curls can be shampooed and conditioned without losing their shape, according to the experts—if they were done correctly in the first place.

2
SKIN

THE SKIN TELLS MANY STORIES about the health and condition of your body, and often about your emotions and your state of mind. Since your skin covers your entire body, it's hard to conceal its problems. If you aren't eating properly, resting enough, and cleaning your body carefully or are experiencing severe psychological problems, effects will probably show up somewhere on your skin, in the form of rashes, blotches, pimples, dryness, or oiliness.

A knowledge of certain basic facts about the skin is crucial to proper skin care. The skin consists of three layers: the hypodermis, a loose layer of connective tissue beneath the dermis, in many areas consisting of subcutaneous fatty tissue; the dermis, site of sweat glands, nerves, blood vessels, smooth muscles, hair follicles, sebaceous glands (which secrete sebum, a colorless, odorless, oily substance that keeps the skin supple), and the blood capillaries that bring oxygen and other indispensable commodities to the skin; and the epidermis, the visible surface of the skin, designed by nature specifically to withstand the effects of the environment. The epidermis constantly renews itself, replacing an entire layer of

21

skin cells with new cells at least once every thirty days. Another important component of the epidermis is a water-attracting compound called the natural moisturizing factor (NMF), which allows the skin to hydrate itself. The amount of NMF in the skin decreases with age—one reason why skin tends to get drier as one gets older.

Skin color is determined by pigment, which is in turn derived from melanin (the Greek word for black), a protein that is produced in everyone's skin by cells called melanocytes. Melanin is the cause of the striking variations in skin color among races as well as within them. Besides determining skin color, melanin also provides protection from the damaging, potentially deadly ultraviolet rays of the sun—extremely important for our ancestors who lived in Africa, where the sun's radiation is intense.

THE ADVANTAGES OF BLACK SKIN

Most experts agree that black skin confers a number of advantages, dermatologically speaking. It is more resistant to all forms of skin cancer; it forms a natural protection against the ultraviolet rays of the sun; and it is more resistant to wrinkling, because it has larger and more numerous oil glands.

CLEANSING

Proper cleansing of the skin is the most crucial element of skin care. It will take you a few extra minutes daily to do the job carefully and thoroughly, but the results will be well worth it. First, know your skin type, since each requires a special cleansing ingredient. A skin-care specialist or dermatologist can tell you your skin type.

Mike Fields

Keep in mind that many experts are opposed to the use of soap, because the alkaloids in it dry out the skin. Others suggest that you use a very mild soap sparingly, making sure to rinse thoroughly. For normal skin, it is recommended that you use a facial milk cleanser followed by a skin freshener or astringent. For dry skin, use a facial cleanser, a skin freshener, and some form of vitamin A and D cream. For oily skin, use a facial cleanser and a nongreasy astringent. For combination dry-and-oily skin, use the above items for dry and oily areas as needed. On all types of skin, a moisturizing lotion should be used after cleansing.

Skin fresheners and astringents should be applied with cotton balls, working with upward and outward strokes, to keep facial tissues from sagging. Avoid the use of washcloths, which tend to leave dirt on the face.

As part of the cleaning process, get in the habit of doing

short facial exercises, such as blowing up the cheeks, squinting the eyes, and exercising the neck, up, down, and around. The stimulation increases circulation and brings new life to skin cells.

SCRUBS

To give the skin a healthier look by hastening the removal of dead outer cells from the surface, try a scrub. Use an abrasive cleanser (a soap with hard particles milled into the bar, or beads or grains in liquid, lotion, or gel bases), applying it with a brush or a loofah and working with circular motions during a warm bath or shower.

Remember that if used too roughly, a scrub can actually cause bleeding. Scrub vigorously, but not crazily. A scrub can be used daily if you use it correctly and if your skin isn't too sensitive; but on the face, because of its extra sensitivity, such brush stimulation should be limited to twice weekly.

COMPLEXION PROBLEMS

The major skin problem confronting black men is the razor bumps that can result from shaving. In medical language they have the formidable name of pseudo folliculitis barbae (PFB). Over 60 percent of black males must contend with PFB at some time in their lives. This potentially scarring skin condition develops when needle-sharp tips of recently shaved hairs curl back and penetrate the skin, thereby creating infectious lumps and bumps. As you might expect, men with the tightly curled hair characteristic of blacks are more prone to PFB than are men with straight hair.

Mike Fields

The most effective way to deal with PFB is to stop shaving and grow a beard. It has been demonstrated that by allowing the beard to grow, the ingrown hairs can ultimately be forced from their pseudo folliculitis. If, however, a beard is impractical or impossible, then you must take certain precautions when shaving. First soak your face with water, using a wet cloth to loosen up the hair shafts. A tooth brush or abrasive sponge can also be used

for this purpose. When shaving, be very careful not to stretch the skin, which may make shaving easier but may also cause the hairs to curl back into the skin. Shave *with* the grain.

Chemical depilatories may be used instead of shaving, but the directions for proper use must be followed diligently because of their potential for skin irritation.

New York hair and skin specialist Nathan Busch has developed a treatment for razor bumps and other problems that result from the shaving of extremely sensitive skin. He uses a mixture of two herbs, golden seal and myrrh, with boiling water. The mixture is allowed to settle until it is cool enough to put on the skin; then it is applied to the inflamed areas with gauze or cotton compresses and allowed to remain until it cools. The application is repeated, after which the skin is thoroughly rinsed with cold water. Finally another herb, pure aloe leaf, is applied and covered with a moisturizer. Ask your dermatologist about this treatment for irritated or inflamed skin.

Another skin problem that confronts many black men is keloids, a condition that occurs when scar tissue, which forms after an injury, continues to form after the injury has been adequately repaired. Normally, in response to an injury, which can be something as minor as a shaving cut or a pimple, the body forms just enough scar tissue to smooth it over. With keloids the injury heals, but the scar becomes gnarled and unsightly, spreading beyond the bounds of the original injury. Certain areas of the body—the neck, jawline, chest, and upper back—are more prone to keloids than are others. Though most people seem to get them in their twenties, keloids can occur in childhood. A four-year-old developed one after having her ears pierced.

Three types of treatment are now available for keloids: removal by excision; X-rays; and the injection of medica-

Mike Fields

tions called corticosteroids, which shrink keloids. Another medication, madacassol, has been used with some success by a French doctor but is not available in the United States.

The causes of keloids are still unknown, and there are no preventive measures known to be effective against them. Until you develop one, there's no way of knowing if you are susceptible to them. They can be treated only after they have formed. Keloids occur more often among blacks and Orientals than among whites. Why this is so isn't known.

Like black women, black men are subject to such skin conditions as darker patches, lighter patches, and ashiness. With darker patches, which are irreversible, perfectly normal, and permanent, the only thing to do is to avoid increasing their size by avoiding friction caused by rubbing elbows, knees, and buttocks on hard surfaces such as desks, chairs, and floors. With lighter patches, which result from traumas to the skin caused by pimples and scratching, the best thing to do is to leave surface eruptions alone as much as possible. The condition usually fades after about a year if it is the result of a minor injury. For ashiness, which is caused by the skin's rapid loss of moisture, a moisturizing cream or lotion should be applied and the skin allowed to absorb it naturally, without rubbing.

Other skin problems, such as whiteheads, blackheads, and acne, occur when the pores of the skin are plugged with an overabundance of the oily-waxy secretion known as sebum. Instead of flowing out onto the surface of the skin, the excess oil clogs the skin, and complexion problems develop. If it were possible to keep the skin unclogged, these particular problems would be virtually nonexistent. Washing the face regularly can help to reduce plug formations and eliminate excess oiliness. Because an injury to the skin from trying to remove a whitehead or pimple can cause a keloid formation, it is highly recommended that you consult your physician or a dermatologist on how to rid yourself of whiteheads, pimples, and acne and then meticulously follow instructions.

Ditto for other skin disorders, such as eczema (an itchy inflammation of the skin) and psoriasis (a chronic inflammatory disease characterized by dry, scaling patches and reddened skin). Don't try home remedies, advice from friends, or products you see advertised. Consult your physician or a dermatologist.

3
BODY CARE

BATHS AND SHOWERS

How many times, as youngsters, did we groan at those terrifying words from Mama, "It's time to take a bath!" Words that rated right up there with dental checkups and castor oil. As we grew older, however, it became a bit clearer what our mothers had in mind. They were trying to establish good health habits in us, habits that would be important to the healthy development of our bodies. As adults we know it's vital—and pleasurable—to hit the shower or jump in the tub to remove grime and perspiration and relax tired muscles after a day at work or at play.

To bathe or to shower, that's the question. Though most men have a preference, it's good to be aware that baths are more drying to the skin. Bath oils aren't essential, but the oil does form a protective film that fights dehydration. Many skin experts recommend a washcloth or a sponge, except on the face, to stimulate the skin and remove surface dead cells while bathing or showering.

One of the main reasons why we bathe or shower is to

keep body odor in check. If, soon after taking a bath or shower, you detect an odor, you may be using the wrong soap. Try an antibacterial deodorant type, but remember that such a soap is not good for all parts of the body. Never use a deodorant soap on your face.

After toweling dry, try a body splash to refresh the body and make it tingle. An oil or a body lotion is helpful to lubricate dry skin and create a fine layer of protection against moisture loss. If you have a serious skin problem, such as excessively dry skin or eczema, your dermatologist can recommend the proper bath products for you.

DEODORANTS AND ANTIPERSPIRANTS

Perspiration is a necessary body function, and a little understanding of it will go a long way in helping you control body odor.

The eccrine glands, whose primary function is to regulate the temperature of the body, and the apocrine glands, which are stimulated by sex hormones and emotional stress, are the two kinds of glands that carry perspiration. While eccrine sweat is mostly salt water and contains almost no organic matter on which bacteria can thrive, apocrine sweat is rich in bacteria that triggers odor-forming action. These bacteria thrive best in warm, moist, well-protected places, such as the underarms and the groin.

The best approach to preventing body odor is bathing daily. It's the best basic way to remove bacteria and glandular secretions. Deodorants are supposed to diminish body odor; however, depending on their ingredients, they may or may not. Most experts agree that, more than anything else, deodorants simply mask odors. Antiperspirants, on the other hand, are intended to inhibit perspiration itself—though most experts agree that nothing can completely stop an individual from sweating even for just a few hours.

If you perspire heavily, whatever you use, deodorant or antiperspirant, will become diluted much more quickly. If, for this reason, you have to use a deodorant or antiperspirant more than once during the day, your skin may become irritated. If this happens, try a different product.

Remember, deodorants are not intended to stop perspiration, but merely to mask body odor with their pronounced fragrance. Antiperspirants delay the delivery of perspiration to the skin's surface; they all contain some type of aluminum salt. The best thing for the groin area is a talc, which will absorb moisture and inhibit bacterial growth.

THE USE OF SCENTS

The way a man smells can be a vital part of his attractiveness, and the effective use of the many scents available today can open up a whole new world.

The first thing to remember is that a cologne becomes "real" only after it's applied to the skin and allowed to react chemically with it. That's why a cologne can smell different on various men. If you have oily skin, the characteristics of a cologne may change dramatically. If you have dry skin, you may have difficulty sustaining a fragrance over a period of time.

For many years men feared they would be considered effeminate if they wore anything other than Old Spice. Those days are over, however, and today the biggest problem is selecting a fragrance from the hundreds on the market—musk, balsam, palm, woodsy, citrus, herbal, spicy, floral, and leather, to name a few.

All colognes have a perfume base, with more perfume essence and alcohol than are in aftershaves, which are less concentrated. The perfume bases consist of essential oils taken mostly from roots, stems, flowers, grasses, foliages, fruits, and spices. The alcohol that makes up most of a cologne's total volume acts as a solvent for these oils.

The cologne or aftershave you choose is entirely up to your personal taste. Just remember never to wear more than one scent at a time. Also be aware that colognes act differently according to the weather. Heat intensifies fragrance, so you may want to wear a lighter scent in summer or if you live in a warm climate.

Don't leave your cologne near a window; light is lethal to cologne. Heat is also an enemy. Try to put the cologne back in its package after each use to retard deterioration.

Some men like to use a cologne on their face after shaving. Just remember that colognes contain more alcohol than do aftershave lotions, which almost always contain emollients and healing agents that act as mild antiseptics for nicks and cuts. Some men use water to cut the strength of a cologne before using it on their face after shaving, but this practice may still prove dangerous to your skin. If you have sensitive skin, I would suggest that you stick with an aftershave. If you have oily skin, a cologne will act as a mild astringent; but if your skin is dry, a cologne will cause your face to chap more easily. Use the cologne on your wrists or neck rather than your face; it will last longer if applied to places that are not exposed to the elements.

DIET AND NUTRITION

It has been proven that thin is better than overweight. It is better for your heart and it adds years to your life. Hundreds of diet books are available for those who plan to go on a strict diet to lose weight; however, if you are one of these brothers, my advice is to see your doctor and let him give you advice on what you should do. This section will advise you on how to make the most of a well-balanced, moderate diet of proteins, vegetables, fruits, fats, and dairy products.

Everything we eat belongs to five food "families," or groups. Nutrients in these foods fit together like pieces of a puzzle to help compose a picture of a sound and healthy

HOLLAND JR. HIGH SCHOOL
MEDIA CENTER

body. Knowing which foods contain which nutrients is the first step toward eating a balanced diet. Eating foods with more calories, or food energy, than we can use means a weight gain. So it is a good general rule to choose most foods from the groups that supply nutrients as well as calories. The four groups that do that are fruits and vegetables; breads and cereals; milk and cheese; and meat, poultry, fish, and beans. The fifth group, fats and sweets, provides lots of calories but few nutrients.

Fruits and vegetables are good sources of vitamin A, vitamin C, and fiber. Vitamin A helps keep the skin healthy. It protects against night blindness and helps you see well. Vitamin A also helps the body grow. Vitamin C builds the material that connects the body's cells. The body needs it for healthy gums and to resist infection. Fiber, some experts say, may help prevent constipation and some diseases of the large intestine. It may also help control your weight. Different fruits and vegetables will give different amounts of these and other nutrients, so it is a good idea to vary the ones you eat. Dark green and deep yellow vegetables such as squash, carrots, broccoli, and greens, provide vitamin A. Most dark green vegetables also supply vitamin C, but only if they are not over-cooked. Citrus fruits such as oranges and grapefruits give lots of vitamin C. Some greens—collard, kale, mustard, turnip, and dandelion—provide calcium and iron, as well as vitamins. Nearly all fruits and vegetables are low in fat, and none has cholesterol unless animal fat is added in cooking.

Enriched breads and cereals, especially whole-grain products, are important sources of the B vitamins, iron, and fiber. They also supply some protein—a good thing to remember if you are cutting down on meat or do not eat it. The B vitamins help our bodies grow at a normal rate. Most breakfast cereals have added nutrients. Some vitamins (for instance, vitamins A, B$_{12}$, C, and D) are added that are not naturally found in cereals. You can find out which nutrients are in a cereal by reading the nutrition label on the box. Foods included among breads and cereals are whole-grain and enriched breads, biscuits, muffins, waffles, pancakes, cooked and ready-to-eat cereals, cornmeal, flour, grits, macaroni and spaghetti, noodles, rice, oats, barley, bulgar, and corn and flour tortillas.

Milk and milk products supply most of the calcium in the average American diet. Milk and its products also give vitamin A and protein. Most milk you buy has vitamin D added to it. Calcium is the mineral that builds teeth and bones. Vitamin D helps your body absorb the calcium you need. You can buy milk in many forms: whole, skim, lowfat, evaporated, buttermilk, and nonfat dry milk. Milk products include yogurt, ice cream, ice milk, and cheeses, including cottage cheese. If you or members of your family prefer the taste of whole milk but not the calories it contains, try mixing it half and half with skim milk or nonfat dry milk and water, made according to the package directions.

Meat, poultry, fish, and beans are important sources of protein, iron, and other minerals and vitamins. Protein is vital to all living cells and helps build and repair body tissues, such as skin, bone, hair, blood, and muscle. Iron helps maintain healthy blood. Because each food offers different combinations of nutrients, try to eat a variety of the foods in this group. Lean, red meats not only give protein, but they supply iron and several of the B vitamins. Liver and egg yolks are valuable sources of vitamin A. Dry peas and beans, soybeans, and nuts supply magnesium, which helps your body change food into energy. Fish and poultry are excellent because they are relatively low in calories and fat but high in vitamins and minerals. Foods in this group include beef, veal, lamb, pork, poultry, fish, shellfish, organ meats (such as liver and kidneys), dry beans and peas, soybeans, lentils, eggs, seeds, nuts, peanuts, and peanut butter. All meat contains cholesterol. Fish and shellfish, except shrimp, are relatively low in cholesterol. Egg yolks and organ meats have the most cholesterol.

Fats and sweets are high in calories and low in nutrients. They should be eaten very moderately and only once in a while if you are trying to lose weight. Fats and oils, for example, have more than twice the calories, ounce for ounce, of protein, starches, or sugars. Calories are food energy, and our bodies need them. The number of calories we need depends on many factors, such as how much energy we use, our growth, and our body size. However, eating more than the body needs will cause you to gain weight. Older people need fewer calories than younger people. Active people need more calories than people who are less active. Men usually need more calories than women. Teenagers need more calories than young children. Foods in this high-calorie group include butter, margarine, lard, dripping, mayonnaise and other salad dressings, other fats and oils, candy, sugar, jams, jellies, many gravies, syrups, sweet toppings, and soft drinks. Also included are bakery products that are not enriched with vitamins and added nutrients. If you are gaining unwanted weight, the foods in this group are the ones to cut down on or cut out. If you still gain weight, eat smaller amounts of foods from the other four groups, but do eat foods from all four. They provide the nutrients our bodies need.

People who eat a lot of animal fat may develop higher levels of the fatlike substance in the blood called cholesterol. Some scientists believe high cholesterol levels are associated with heart disease. Too much cholesterol in the blood can cause fat to build up and block the blood's passage through the arteries. The fats you eat come from two sources—animals and vegetables. Fats are naturally present in such foods from animals as whole milk, cheese, and meat. Fats from vegetables are in nuts and chocolate. Fats are naturally present in some foods. In others, we add fats and oil in cooking, such as in fried foods, pastries, some gravies, and salad dressings. If you think your diet may include too much fat and you want to cut down, here are some suggestions:

Include more fruits and vegetables, whole-grain breads, cereals, and dry beans and peas in your meals. Eat lean meats rather than fatty ones. Don't eat the skins of poultry. Do include more fish and the meat of chicken and turkey and other poultry in your meals; they are generally low in fat. Watch the amount of nuts, peanuts, and peanut butter; they have a lot of protein, but they also have a lot of fat. Use skim or low-fat milk and their products instead of whole milk and its products. Ice milk, for example, has less fat than ice cream. Uncreamed cottage cheese has less fat than the creamed kind.

You don't have to do all these things. For instance, if you cut down on your meat fat, you don't have to worry as much about the fat in milk. The idea is to avoid extremes.

Sugar and most sweets don't offer you much more than calories. When you eat a lot of them, they are likely to take the place of foods that offer more in vitamins, minerals, and protein. Experts agree that eating too much sugar speeds tooth decay and may add unwanted pounds. It's hard to be sure how much sugar you actually eat, because some foods come with sugar already added.

Here are some points to keep in mind:

Check the labels. Remember that ingredients are listed by the amount the product contains. If sugar is listed first, the product contains more sugar than anything else. If it is second or third, it contains more sugar than all but one or two other ingredients. And so on down the list. Maybe the label won't say "sugar." Watch for such terms as sucrose, glucose, dextrose, fructose, corn syrups, corn sweeteners, natural sweeteners, and invert sugars. They are all forms of sugar. Many dentists say that for better and healthier teeth, you should eat less sugar and sweet foods; instead of sweets between meals, eat fresh fruits and vegetables. Brush or rinse your mouth after meals or snacks, especially when you have had sweet foods. Drink more water and fruit juices and fewer soft drinks, fruit drinks, soda pop, and punches, most of which have lots of sugar. Go easy on candy, pies, cakes, pastries, and cookies. Buy fruit canned in its own juice or in light syrup. Many cereals come with sugar already added. If you buy cereal without sugar, you can add the amount of sugar you want. But if it's already there, you can't scrape it off. Keep temptation out of easy reach; don't keep the sugar bowl on the table where you eat.

So you still want to be sexy and slim? Believe me, it's not easy. But for those of you who are determined, let's go on to something we are all guilty of: snacking our way to bigness. Is it true what they say about snacking? That it's bad for you and you shouldn't do it? Ever? Well, yes. And then again, no. The answer depends on how much you eat at meals and what food you choose for snacks. Snacks can be a great idea if they give your body the nutritious foods that your regular meals are lacking. Some people can't or don't want to eat a lot at one sitting. They may get hungry before it's time for the next meal.

There is nothing wrong with feeding your body at times other than meal time. But you shouldn't overload on calories or gobble up snacks that are loaded with sugar, salt, and fat. Many people would rather substitute a later snack for a dessert at meals. Fine, if your calorie count will permit it. Nutritious snack foods include fruits and fruit juices, custards or puddings, yogurt, homemade popcorn (easy on the oil), and breadsticks.

EVERYDAY ACTIVITY

All summer, our parks are filled with the young and the not-so-young, jogging, playing paddleball, handball, soft-ball, and basketball. Visit any beach and you'll find people swimming and splashing in the ocean. During the winter, the health clubs do big business. All of these people have one objective in mind: to keep in shape.

Mike Fields

Keeping in shape is vital. Everything you do depends on your health and the state of your body. You take a big chance when you neglect your body all winter and try to get it in shape overnight for summer. It's important that you give some time to keeping the body in general good care all year long.

There are many things you can do at home to keep the body in shape. A balanced program should do the following things: strengthen and tone muscles, stimulate the cardiovascular system, increase flexibility, and develop coordination. To achieve these things, involve yourself in a well-paced series of muscle-isolation exercises that work on particular groups of muscles. A good exercise program will boost your energy level. You will know that the exercise is working when you begin to feel the results. To get the maximum effect of any exercise, breathe deeply and regularly throughout your workout, concentrate on the muscle group you are exercising, and keep your stomach tucked in and tight at all times.

Exercise improves the general fitness of your body, as well as its appearance. Once you start your exercise program, you must maintain discipline. Do not start and stop, and remember—start slowly, especially if you are starting a new program or if you have not been at it for a while. Here is a partial list of things you can do on your own and at home that will benefit your body:

Calisthenics. Calisthenics consume body energy, which makes them helpful in losing weight. Sit-ups strengthen abdominal muscles. Push-ups work on the torso and upper arms. Calisthenics also increase endurance, as well as size. Body parts become more flexible and agile.

Jogging. Do not start jogging until you have a "stress check" that can pinpoint silent heart disease if you are over thirty-five. Remember that sudden exercise can throw heart rhythm out of sync. Jogging does strengthen

the heart, which in turn can pump more blood with less effort. But before you really get into jogging, make sure your heart can handle it.

Walking. Walking can also help strengthen the heart and tone the body. That doesn't mean that if you take a leisurely walk for a couple of blocks once a week you have it made. Walk at a healthy speed; a leisurely stroll does little for you.

Weight lifting. Weight lifting does nothing for general fitness of the body, but it does increase physical strength and muscle size.

Cycling. Like jogging, cycling helps the heart because it involves sustained, rhythmic, repetitive movements, as well as deep breathing. If you are going to get involved in cycling, remember that rigorous physical activity should be performed on a regular basis. Three or four times a week may be adequate.

Mike Fields

Mike Fields

Dancing. The notion that we all have rhythm is not exactly true. Some of us do and some of us don't. Dancing is a form of exercise that can both be fun and get the job done. It's great for discipline and muscle control. Pro football teams have included dance sessions in their preseason training, because they help the athletes achieve endurance and flexibility. Health clubs use dancing on a regular basis as a way to put fun into exercise.

SPORTS

Here are some popular sports and what they contribute in shaping up your body:

Swimming. If there is one sport that gets the job done, it's swimming. If you are swimming in competition or swimming simply for the pleasure of it, it is the most sustained exercise, since strength, endurance, power, agility, and cardiovascular-respiratory demands are high. Swimming is the best all-around activity for getting and keeping the body in shape. It's also excellent for losing extra pounds. You don't have to qualify for the Olympics; just be able to swim several laps daily.

Basketball. Perhaps the most popular sport among black men, young and not-so-young alike, basketball has al-

Mike Fields

ways been looked upon as the best way to get and stay in shape. Professional football players organize basketball teams in the off-season. Basketball develops the cardio-vascular-respiratory system, endurance, flexibility, and coordination; however, musculature won't be influenced a lot. But basketball is great fun and will improve body function a great deal.

Handball and paddleball. Handball, which is played mostly in the northern cities (especially New York), is a fast-paced all-around activity. Paddleball offers similar benefits. Neither sport increases strength, but each is excellent for general development.

Football. Many young black brothers do their thing either on the basketball court or on the football field. Football, when played on a regular basis, improves muscular endurance but does nothing to increase strength or agility. That is why football players are put on weight-lifting programs to increase their strength.

Baseball. Baseball does nothing to increase strength or agility, but it does improve muscular endurance.

Tennis. Tennis demands stamina and agility. It doesn't build the same amount of physical strength as some other activities, but it can be a lot more exciting.

4
HANDS AND FEET

HAND CARE

Believe it or not, your hands tell a lot about you. They reveal self-confidence and assurance, as well as how you feel about yourself. Have you ever shaken hands with someone and felt as if you were holding a limp dishcloth? That person didn't make a good impression on you, did he? Attractive hands are important in any situation, especially when you're looking for a job or want to make an impression on someone. Bitten fingernails and rough, scaly skin will turn people off just as quickly as bad breath.

Well-groomed hands are a very definite asset to a man in all social situations. Hands are important to women. Some women get their impressions about men by looking at their hands. If a man is strong-willed and at ease with himself, his hands will look strong and his handshake will be firm. Sexual messages are conveyed by simple gestures of the hands.

Give your hands as much attention as you do other

parts of your body. If you don't have the time or don't know how to take care of your nails, spend five or six dollars and get them done by a professional. However, if you want to do them yourself, wait till after a bath or shower.

Here are the steps to take in manicuring your nails:

1. Cut your nails short and in conformance with the curve of the fingertips, using a simple clipper or scissors.

2. To file, use an emery board; it's easier on the nails than a metal file.

3. Smooth the rough edges by filing from the sides toward the center; file in one direction only.

4. If your cuticles are sufficiently softened, gently push them back with a cotton swab or with the towel as you dry your hands.

5. Clean your nails thoroughly with a nail brush to remove as much cuticle as you can from the nail surface.

6. If the cuticles are ragged, clip them with nail scissors.

7. Clean under the nails with an orangewood stick.

If you have dry skin, wear gloves in winter to prevent chapping and ashiness. Also use an oil or lotion to replace lost moisture and make your hands more attractive.

FOOT CARE

Here are some facts you should know about your feet:

～ Each foot contains:
  26 bones
  38 joints
  Yards of fiber and blood vessels
  A complete network of muscles and ligaments

~ Feet are flexible, durable, and strong: The average person's feet will walk about 115,000 miles in a lifetime! Because feet are a sensitive area of the body and because people spend from 75 to 80 percent of their waking hours on their feet, keeping your feet strong, comfortable, and healthy is important to your physical and mental health. The feet affect the alignment of the whole skeletal system, so that being able to move and walk freely adds to your entire sense of well-being.

~ 98 percent of all people are born with normal feet. But most people develop problems. By the age of two, many children develop foot defects or suffer damage; by adulthood most people suffer from some foot disorder.

To avoid some of these problems, take the following precautions when buying shoes:

1. Choose and wear proper shoes; *do not* choose a shoe because it looks handsome or is fashionable. A shoe should be chosen because it feels as well as it looks on your feet.

2. Try shoes on (manufacturers' sizes differ). Have your feet measured while standing each time you buy shoes.

3. Fit the larger foot first. Everyone has one foot that is larger than the other.

4. Allow room between the end of the longest toe and the tip of the shoe; usually a thumbnail width is sufficient.

5. The ball of the foot should fit snugly into the widest part of the shoe.

6. Be sure to buy shoes that are comfortable. Never buy shoes you have to break in.

7. Examine shoes for quality (look for strength, smooth stitching, finished edges, and durability).

8. Uncomfortable styles and extremes should be avoided (very high heels, platforms, clogs, and so on).

9. Select shoes made of leather or fabric, both of which conform to the shape of the foot and allow the foot to breathe; synthetics do not. Also, leather soles resist puncture.

General Foot Care

Good foot hygiene should be practiced daily. Wash your feet thoroughly, including between each toe, and dry them carefully, making sure also to dry between your toes.

Use an absorbent foot powder to keep your feet dry.

Trim your toenails carefully: cut nails straight across, and be careful not to cut toenails too short! The nails should be slightly longer than the tips of the toes.

Avoid home remedies. Do not treat your own corns, calluses, or ingrown nails. Harsh medications or chemical compounds (so-called corn cures) should also be avoided. Seek professional advice for these problems, as well as for burns, cuts, frostbite, and breaks in the skin.

Basic Foot Problems

Corns are small, circular hard areas, usually located on top of a toe above the center joint. Corns are usually caused by friction and pressure resulting from deformities. TREATMENT: Relieve pressure by wearing properly fitted shoes; see a podiatrist for advice and treatment. Avoid over-the-counter "corn cures," which may aggravate the problem.

Calluses are areas of hard, thickened skin, appearing

most frequently on the heel or the ball of the foot. Calluses are generally caused by friction and pressure on the areas affected. TREATMENT: Avoid the source of stress. Sometimes this problem can be treated by balancing the foot with an orthotic device.

Flat feet are feet without arches. They can be painful or even crippling. Flat feet can be inborn or can result from an injury, especially to ligaments or other tissues of the feet. TREATMENT: Arch supports (orthotics), corrective shoes, casts, or braces may be prescribed.

Bunions are misaligned joints that become enlarged (swollen) and painful. The joint of the big toe is most often affected, developing an overgrowth of bone. Bunions are caused by muscle imbalance, joint abnormalities, inflammation, or the wearing of shoes that are too narrow. TREATMENT: Cortisone injections or surgery may sometimes be necessary. Special orthotics to control abnormal motions may also be prescribed.

Athlete's foot: starts with tiny blisters that burst and dry up, resulting in brownish-yellow spots, flaking, cracking, itching, burning, and pain. The cause is a fungus infection. TREATMENT: Keep feet clean and dry; use antifungal powder or cream. It may be necessary to consult a podiatrist if the problem is persistent.

Ingrown toenails are toenails whose corners dig painfully into the skin. The cause is usually improper nail cutting, but they can also be caused by inherited factors, injury, or fungus infection. TREATMENT: Soak affected foot. See a podiatrist for early treatment to prevent infection. Surgery may be necessary.

Gout is a metabolic disorder causing chronic pain in and swelling of a joint, most often that of a big toe. The cause is a disturbance of uric-acid metabolism. This condition can be aggravated by improperly fitting shoes, alcohol, and certain foods. TREATMENT: Your podiatrist or physician may prescribe medication for treatment of the underlying disease.

Contact dermatitis is an inflammation of the skin characterized by burning, itching, redness, and sometimes small red bumps, or water blisters. The cause is usually an allergic reaction to such substances as soap, powders, sprays, or shoe materials. TREATMENT: Avoid the offending substance if you can identify it yourself, or seek an accurate diagnosis from a podiatrist or dermatologist. Improper self-treatment can seriously worsen the condition.

Foot strain is a dull, pulsating ache in the arch of the foot, which sometimes feels as if the foot is breaking apart. This condition is caused by stress and fatigue. TREATMENT: Massage, soaking in hot water, and rest may help; foot strapping and orthotics (arch supports) may be required.

Foot Cramps are sudden, severe cramps in the arch that usually occur when the foot is relaxed. The cause is uncertain, but is believed to be a chemical build-up in the muscles or a blood-vessel disease. TREATMENT: Stretch the affected muscle and knead it until the cramps end (usually a matter of minutes).

Burning feet is a sensation commonly felt in the soles of the feet. This condition is generally caused by a disturbance in the sensory nerves, usually related to overweight, alcoholism, diabetes, or synthetics in the shoes. TREATMENT: An adequate diet rich in B vitamins often helps. Alcohol must be avoided, as must synthetics in shoes.

Plantar warts are warts that painfully penetrate the sole of the foot, surrounding themselves with dead tissue. The cause is a contagious virus. TREATMENT: Warts should be removed, as they can spread and multiply if not treated. Warts of the foot should be treated by a podiatrist or dermatologist.

Fashion

5
THE BASIC PRINCIPLES OF GOOD DRESS

MEN'S FASHION TODAY is more changeable than at any other time in modern history. For years women's fashions changed almost monthly, while men could count on styles lasting at least two seasons. But no more. What's in today may very well be out tomorrow. With blacks especially, it seems fads are born every day. Some remain longer than others—some for years. The dashiki is one example. The wide-brimmed hat popularized by former Knick superstar Walt "Clyde" Frazier is another.

But although most black men in America were for the statement that the dashiki and other styles made during the sixties, every look was not for every man. Black men, especially young black men, have been greatly influenced, first by black entertainers and later by black pro athletes, in their dress and grooming—but here again, not every trend is for every man. The key principle of good dress is to choose styles that best suit both your physical type and your personality. Remember, it's not what you wear, but how you wear it, that makes the difference.

Good dress is more than wearing the right accessories

with the right suit or having your hair neatly cut. It is also wearing the correct attire for the occasion. A young brother who wears a ski suit and cap to a dance when the occasion calls for a dress suit is not dressed properly. Same thing when you and your date have tickets to a Broadway show and you show up in jeans and sneakers. So you should not only select clothes that suit you, but you should also wear them at the right times. Remember that your clothes should complement you, not supplant you. Someone once said that "those who make their dress a principal part of themselves will in general become of no more value than their dress."

PERSONALITY

Before you can decide what clothes are best for your personality, you have to decide just what your personality is.

Many young brothers are openly determined to confront American society as men—black men. They are, as we say, getting it together. To those who have chosen to travel this route, let me say that your personality is the core of what you present to the world. Your total makeup is revealed through your personality. The way you talk,

Mike Fields

the way you walk, the way you dress, how you affect others, how others relate to you, depend on your personality. Most importantly, the things that you project are projections of how you feel about yourself.

There are many facets to an individual's personality. There are times when you want to express yourself differently from other times. Don't panic; there is nothing wrong. Your personality also has contradictions. You have moods, and you find yourself in circumstances where your personality expresses itself in different ways. Your clothes can be one way of expressing those various aspects of yourself. When you see clothes that you feel are not right for you, don't force the issue. If you are not the type of man who wears jeans, don't wear jeans simply to please someone else.

Mike Fields

There's a lot to think about in dressing for your private and business lives, yet the guidelines are really fairly simple, involving more logic than law. Let your image be specific. Having a specific image gives those around you the feeling that they know you.

When in doubt as to whether to go all out, don't. It's best to dress down and wait for that special time when excessiveness is in the air. Call as much attention to yourself as you can handle, but no more. Remember that you are going to be evaluated on a number of things, with tradition at one end and innovation at the other. Again, take into account your own personality and the nature of the occasion at hand.

DRESSING THE PHYSICAL YOU

As important as knowing what styles to wear when is making sure the fit and colors of your clothes best complement your body type and coloring. The following should provide some useful hints.

The Stocky Man

Suits and sport jackets. Since your abdominal region is more pronounced, your jacket should have lightly padded shoulders and minimal waist suppression. The jacket should not be too long. Let as much leg show as possible to help give the look of height; try a two-button model. Fabric should have a vertical design or a small subdued pattern. Avoid bright colors; medium to dark colors are more slimming. Peaked lapels work better than shawl or notched. Avoid a jacket with a belt, since it draws attention to the waist. Avoid also close hip-fitting or flared jackets, which accentuate the behind. Try side vents and a slightly loose-fitting jacket.

Shirts. More than likely a stocky man will have a short neck, which means the collar of his shirts should be low. Collar points should be short to medium; a regular spread or tab is best. Avoid tapered shirts, as well as ruffles and other embellishments. Plain and simple is best.

Ties. A narrow tie in a soft pattern is best. Stripes can work when used properly, but don't get carried away. A four-in-hand knot is better than a Windsor. Tie fabric should be medium weight.

Sweaters. Bulky sweaters are best for the stocky male. Choose moderate collars, not those that spread from shoulder to shoulder. Stay away from long sweaters; anything that falls below the waist is bad news. Turtlenecks are not the best, but can be useful if they're bulky.

Vests. Make sure the vest has a V shape, which creates the right frame for the face and gives a slimming look.

Pants. Select plain designs with pleats, which make your hips and waistline seem larger. Leave the legs uncuffed and choose a lightweight fabric. The idea is to get a smooth straight line from waist to feet.

The Tall, Thin Man

Suits and sport jackets. The jacket should have light padding in the shoulder; too much padding, however, will make the tall, thin male look top-heavy. Pay particular attention to your lapels. If they are too wide or too narrow you will look thinner. Moderate lapels will keep the undeveloped chest from being dwarfed. If you have wide shoulders, you can go from moderate to wide in the lapels. Waist suppression should depend on the width of your shoulders and the size of your waist. If you have very wide shoulders and a small waist, only a slight suppression is necessary. Notched lapels are better than

Regular collar.

Spread collar.

Long-pointed collar.

Rounded collar.

Tab collar.

Button-down collar.

peaked lapels on this physique. Double-breasted suits work well; single-breasted styles should have at least a two-button closure. The jacket should have side vents or no vents, which works very well. Avoid pinstripes, which emphasize height and thinness.

Shirts. The key feature in a shirt is the collar. Most tall, thin brothers have long necks that look best in high collars; rounded collars can also work. If your jacket has moderate lapels, a moderate-spread, medium-high collar is another alternative. Make sure the points are not too long; they add to the vertical effect. If you're on the skinny side, a semitapered shirt will give you a fuller look, but avoid a full-cut shirt that takes over the body.

Ties. When selecting your ties, remember that thin does not go with thin; there must be a balance. Avoid especially wide ties, which make your chest look even narrower. Use muted colors as much as possible and stay away from the hot (bright) colors, which draw too much attention. Use a half Windsor knot.

Sweaters. You have a number of sweater styles to select from, but stay away from mock turtleneck if your neck is long. Ditto for scoopnecks, henley necks, and set-in-shoulders. Your best bets are full turtlenecks, collar necks, and cowl necks. Raglan shoulders also work well. Never wear a skinny top with a skinny bottom.

Vests. Since vests are slenderizing, the tall, thin brother has little use for them. If you do wear one, don't let it be one that matches your jacket and pants; a lighter color works better. You can also make good use of the sleeveless sweater as an alternative.

Pants. With this body type, you can wear pleated or unpleated. Long legs look great in the heavier fabrics— woolens, wide-wale corduroys, uncut velvets, and twills. Your pants can have a slight flare. Cuffs are up to you.

The Y-Shaped, or Top-Heavy Man

Suits and sport jackets. Ready-to-wear offers little for the odd sizes. Watch the young black brothers on the street and you'll see the physique of the future: wide shoulders, small waist, long thighs and arms. A man who wears size 42 or 44 long jacket, but whose waist size is 32 or 34, has a serious problem in buying a suit. A simple alteration is out, and he'll be hard pressed to find a retailer who will substitute the pants. The pants must be recut, and the jacket will look baggy unless it's pinched in the waist. These alterations may be costly, but they are worth it so that the suit will fit correctly.

In sport jackets, the idea is to cut down on the shirt exposure. Lapels should be moderate. Choose side vents if you are big in the behind. Shoulder padding is not necessary, since this is an area you're trying to play down.

Shirts. Some Y-shaped men have thick, short necks. If you're one, wear a low-collar shirt. If you have a normal-to-long neck, wear a moderate-height collar. And if your neck is just plain long, try a high collar. Whichever style you choose, your collar should have long points and a narrow spread. Avoid tapered shirts; semitapered is more suitable, because it breaks up your top and bottom and deemphasizes your Y-shaped physique.

Ties. Narrow ties work best. Patterns should be small and subtle, in order not to draw undue attention to this area.

Sweaters. Like the long-point, narrow-spread shirt, a V-neck sweater slenderizes your top. Avoid fancy styles; simplicity is the key. Nothing bulky, please; turtlenecks, mock-turtles, and keyhole necks can work well for you if you select carefully.

Vests. A vest may not always work for you, especially if you are much bigger on top than on the bottom. Vests with low closures or lapels are out. In order to play down the triangular appearance of the shirt, choose a vest with a high closure.

Pants. The idea here is to balance your top and bottom for a better line. The top-heavy physique already has enough top; what you want to do is give your bottom some width. So go berserk with wide straight-leg pants, pleated or unpleated, and wide flares. Choose hefty fabrics; corduroys, cavalry twills, heavy chinos, herringbones, and tweeds will all work well for you. Avoid western-cut jeans and peg-leg pants.

The Pear-Shaped, or Bottom-Heavy, Man

Suits and sport jackets. An overall balance is the key for this body type. Since this brother's waistline will probably be larger than his chest, he should avoid jackets with belts or suppressed waistlines. The same goes for double-breasted suits and jackets that flare. You don't want to draw attention to anything from the waist down. Wear side vents in your jacket, and keep lapels moderate to wide.

Shirts. Choose a shirt with a low collar, medium to wide spread, and moderate points. Clean, simple lines are best; avoid such frills as contrast collars and French cuffs.

Ties. The collar style I recommend for your body type calls for a tie that borders on being wide.

Sweaters. Turtlenecks, crew necks, shawl collars, and V necks work well. Keep sweaters waist length, and stay away from long wraparounds.

Vests. A vest can work well as a trimming device, helping to focus the eyes on the top of the body. A vest in the same tone and fabric as your suit or sport jacket is best.

Pants. High-rise pants are best. Stay away from heavy fabrics, bell bottoms, flares, and western styles.

The Rotund Man

Suits and sport jackets. No suppression in the jacket; double-breasted suits or sport jackets are out. Moderation is important in everything you wear—moderate lapels, color tones, fabrics, and styles. No plaids or tweeds, please. Side vents work best.

Shirts. Medium or low collars with long points and narrow spreads work best.

Ties. Here again, moderation. Your ties should not be too narrow or too wide, too loud or too quiet.

Sweaters. Long wraps and cardigans with belts are out, as are patterns and textured knits. Anything that adds weight is a no-no. Your best shot is a plain V-neck sweater.

Vests. A vest could be the best item in your wardrobe. Remember, for the vest to be used most successfully, it should be of the same fabric and color as the suit or sport jacket. This will give you a slimmer look.

Pants. Wear plain pants with a high rise and straight legs with no hint of a flare.

COLOR COORDINATION

Every black man has a distinctive shade that looks better with some colors than with others. Here are some coordination suggestions for making the best of the basic colors in suits, shirts, and accessories.

The Ideal Fit in a Suit

Shoulders lie straight; no pull.

Waist tapered smoothly at body's natural waistline.

Sleeves expose ½" of shirt cuff, are fuller at the shoulders and taper gently to the wrist.

Collar fits low and snug, exposing ½" of shirt collar.

Lapels rolled low to the middle button.

Lower edge hangs parallel to the floor, covers the seat.

Legs fall straight with no twisting.

Trousers touch the shoe in front without "breaking," reach heel seam in back.

The Dark-Skinned Man

The gray suit. Medium to light shades look best, though you can wear the whole range of gray successfully.

SHIRTS. Since gray is a neutral color, almost anything goes, but your best shirt colors are blue, pink, pale yellow, white, and gold. Solid-color shirts in any of these colors work well, as do stripes: red and white, blue and white, yellow and white, pink and white. If you wear a solid white shirt, take advantage of bold solid-color ties— orange, gold, deep purple, deep blue. Stay away from brown, which works poorly for dark-skinned males.

SHOES. Black leather shoes, of course. If you like wearing shoes of the same color as your suit, choose a darker gray.

ACCESSORIES. You can have a field day with ties because of gray's neutrality. All shades of blue, red, and maroon work well, as do bold shades of gold, purple, plum, and pink. Just make sure your shirt and tie complement each other.

The blue suit. Dark-complected men look best in medium to light shades.

SHIRTS. Most shirt colors mix very well with blue: yellow, blue, white, pink, peach, orange, mauve, mulberry. All work well with your complexion. Light tan can be worn successfully if the blue suit is medium to dark. The idea is to separate your dark complexion from the blue of the suit. So stick with light shades. The solid shirt with white collar is perfect for you. So are striped shirts in red, blue, yellow, or pink.

SHOES. Black leather is the safest bet. Other colors are too difficult to coordinate. In a warm climate or in summer, if you're wearing a lightweight blue suit, you might go with two-tone blue-and-white summer shoes—but never on the job.

ACCESSORIES. You have a large selection in ties: red, maroon, gold, ivory, yellow, blue, burgundy, gray. The white shirt is traditional with the blue suit; wear ties of red, maroon, burgundy, gold, yellow, or blue. With a pastel-colored shirt, a red, burgundy, or maroon tie works very well. Striped, patterned, and floral ties go beautifully with the blue suit. Never, but never, wear a black tie. Even if you wear a dark blue suit to a semiformal affair, select a nice burgundy, a soft red, or a navy blue with a pastel or white shirt.

The tan suit. Medium to light shades are best for you. Tan is not neutral, but it's a good shade for the dark-skinned man. Do not wear tans that border on brown.

SHIRTS. The general idea is not to put anything dark against your skin, so don't wear a dark-tone shirt in an effort to complement your suit. Blue, yellow, maroon, plum, and white solids are good, as are the same colors in stripes. White-collar shirts work well with this suit. The lighter the tan of your suit, the deeper the tone should be in your shirt. That is, deep blue, deep yellow, and so on.

SHOES. Stay in the tan family. If your suit is light tan, shoes should be medium to dark tan. If the suit is medium to dark, shoes can be light. Never wear black or pastel colors. The only way to use brown (if it's a golden shade) is with a white shirt and solid brown tie (or a pattern with brown in it). Even then, stay away from the brown tones with a lot of black in them.

ACCESSORIES. If your shirt is solid, wear a patterned tie in which orange, red, yellow, tan, blue, or burgundy is

dominant. If you wear a solid tie, try red on a blue shirt, burgundy on a yellow shirt. With blue, red, burgundy, and maroon shirts with white stripes, your best bets are solid ties of orange or soft yellow. Don't wear a tie the same color as your shirt. There must be a definite contrast. A brown tie is not the best for your complexion, but it can be worn successfully with a white shirt. However, stay with the lighter shades of brown. With two-tone shirts, let your tie complement the color of the body of the shirt; you can use deeper tones here because the white collar will separate your dark complexion from the tone of your shirt.

The white or eggshell suit. A good shade for the dark-skinned man, especially in warm climates.

SHIRTS. The white suit allows you to expand your choice of shirt colors; it's hard to be wrong when coordinating this color. Try blue, burgundy, maroon, yellow, soft lavender, plum, blue with white stripes, red with white stripes, burnt orange, and two-tone pale blue, red, and burgundy.

SHOES. White, tan, eggshell, or off-white are the best shades for this suit. Stay away from pastels—lavender, red, yellow. Wear brown only if you wear a brown tie and a white shirt; it's not your best combination for this suit, but it's not too bad.

ACCESSORIES. If your shirt is solid, wear a patterned, striped, or floral tie. With a blue shirt, your tie should have some yellow or red in it, or a combination of both. With a soft burgundy shirt, your tie should have tones of red, yellow, orange, or gold. A blue shirt with white stripes works well with ties of solid blue, burgundy, burnt orange, or yellow. Ties with small patterns in which these colors are dominant can also be used. A red shirt with white stripes will allow you to wear a solid red, white, maroon, blue, or burgundy tie. Small patterns where these colors are present can also be used.

The Brown-Skinned Man

The brown suit. Medium to light shades are best. Dark browns can be worn successfully, but be careful with blackish browns.

SHIRTS. White and tan are the safest colors. Yellow, peach, and pink can also work very well, especially if the brown is medium to dark. Light blue, pink, or red stripes can be considered, as can all of the plum shades. If the suit is almost tan, your best shirt colors are deep blue, light burgundy, red, or blue stripes; brown is fine if it's not too dark.

SHOES. Brown leather if the suit is close to tan. If the suit is a true brown, try shoes of red-brown, blue-brown, golden-brown, or olive-brown. I would recommend staying away from black shoes altogether.

ACCESSORIES. Brown ties are naturals with tannish suits; either harmonizing or contrasting is good. With a true brown suit, try ties of ivory, tan, gold, yellow, or light gray. For tan suits, striped and patterned ties should have a combination of brown, yellow, gold, white, burgundy, or red; brown suits work well with ties combining ivory, tan, gold, yellow, light gray, or white. You can wear a solid brown tie with a brown suit, but your shirt should be white, yellow, or peach. Depending on the color of your shirt, a white tie can also be interesting.

The blue suit. As we've said, blue works well with most complexions. The brown-skinned man, however, can take advantage of a wider range of shades than can the dark-skinned or fair-skinned man.

SHIRTS. Although almost any shirt color can work with blue, the best colors for your complexion are orange, white, yellow, pink, peach, and gray. Blue, red, mulberry, and pale burgundy may also work. Two-tone solid shirts make it easy for you to accessorize the blue suit to the max. The striped shirt—blue and white, red and white, burgundy and white—gives another dimension to the blue suit. Whatever you do, never wear a brown shirt; it rarely comes out right.

SHOES. Black leather is your best bet. Never wear brown. Your alternative is the blue and white two-tone—especially good with a lightweight summer suit.

ACCESSORIES. You have a wide selection of ties with the blue suit. With a dark blue suit, try a white or pale blue

shirt and a tie of gold, burgundy, red, orange, or plum. Other tie colors that work well for you are ivory, maroon, and mauve.

The white, eggshell, or antique suit. Always striking on the brown-skinned man.

SHIRTS. Almost any shirt color will complement this suit. For your complexion, some good choices are: deep blue, gold, pale red or burgundy, peach pink, yellow, the plum shades, and lavender. Striped shirts of red, blue, brown, and burgundy will be very effective. Be very careful with a solid brown; the color should be medium to light. If it's too dark, it will fade into your complexion. You can use a tan shirt effectively if you wear a brown tie. Stay away from white. A two-tone shirt (white collar with striped or solid body) can work if the dominant color is right.

SHOES. Black is out for this color suit. Brown is your number-one color: reddish-brown, golden-brown, grayish-brown, and so on. Also great for your complexion: brown and white, blue and white, and burgundy and white two-tones.

ACCESSORIES. Here, too, you have a wide selection in ties: deep blues, gold, brown, red, burgundy, purple, orange, and sometimes white. This is an easy suit to coordinate for your complexion. A deep blue tie on a pale blue striped shirt works especially well; try blue and white two-tone shoes.

The Light-Brown Skinned Man

The gray suit. Although you can wear the whole range of gray, charcoal is your best color. Medium to light shades can be worn successfully with the correct accessories.

SHIRTS. You have a wide selection of shirts with the gray suit: blue, white, gold, yellow, pink, and even gray if the

shirt is lighter than the suit. I wouldn't suggest a dark gray shirt if the suit is charcoal; however, with a very light gray suit, a dark gray shirt can be an interesting choice. Stay away from olive, red, maroon, and brown shirts with the darker gray suit. These shades work nicely with lighter shades of gray.

SHOES. Black leather is really your only choice.

ACCESSORIES. Nearly all tie colors work with gray—all shades of blue, deep reds, maroons, burgundy. Patterns or stripes with gold, burgundy, white, red, maroon, gold, or tan add brightness to a dark gray background.

The brown suit. Medium to dark shades are best. Tan has a tendency to look washed out.

SHIRTS. White or blue are safe for your complexion.

Avoid pale colors; a good tone is necessary next to your skin for contrast. Try deep shades of pink, gold, and orange. Solid shirts with white collars are a good bet, as are stripes of brown and white or orange and white. Brown and white stripes can be tricky, so be careful. If you do wear a tan suit, make sure your shirt is a deep shade. A solid here would be best.

SHOES. Brown leather is best.

ACCESSORIES. Make use of striped and patterned ties. Try mixtures of white, gold, blue, ivory, brown, and yellow. A solid brown tie can work with a white, deep gold, or pink shirt.

The blue suit. You can wear the whole range of blue, but your best shades are medium to dark.

SHIRTS. Most shirt colors are good for blue: white, blue, red, burgundy, pink, peach, maroon, orange, mulberry. Never wear a brown shirt with any shade of blue. Tan is out, because there will be too little contrast between your skin and the shirt. Solid shirts with white collars should work well. So should stripes: blue, red, maroon, burgundy, pink, and mulberry.

SHOES. Black leather is best.

ACCESSORIES. Take advantage of striped and patterned ties. The use of color is very important for your complexion; try mixes of red, white, gold, maroon, burgundy, and yellow. If you go to a solid tie, try maroon, burgundy, or red with a blue or white shirt. Gold with a blue shirt is also quite striking. Never wear a brown tie with a blue suit.

The Fair-Skinned Man

The black suit. The whole range of black, from black-black to charcoal to black with dark gray stripes or patterns, is excellent for your complexion.

SHIRTS. The best choices are tan, white, blue, pale red, and pale burgundy. If you want to go all out: pink, peach, and mauve. Striped shirts with white collars give you even more flexibility, as do two-tone solids.

SHOES. Naturally, black is the first choice. If you like the black-and-brown look, don't wear dark brown; there must be more of a contrast between suit and shoes. Select a medium or light shade.

ACCESSORIES. Try ties in tan, yellow, gold, gray, silver,

rust, blue, red, maroon, and burgundy. If you like the black-and-brown look, try a black suit, white shirt, and medium-brown tie.

The olive suit. The fair-skinned man is best served by the medium to dark shades; although he can wear the lighter shades, they don't always work to his advantage.

SHIRTS. Your selection is limited unless you get into high-fashion colors; the best are white, blue (medium to light), yellow, and tan (if used with the correct shade of olive). If you really want to go all out, try peach, orange, rust, or mauve.

SHOES. Black leather is the best choice. Dark brown shoes can also be worn successfully.

ACCESSORIES. Tie colors to wear with olive: tan, yellow, gold, gray, silver, rust, maroon, and olive itself (make sure there is a contrast between the shades). Blue is excellent for olive, especially when the olive suit has blue in it. However, avoid the lighter shades of blue in ties; they do little for you.

The blue suit. Fair-skinned men look best in the medium and dark shades. The lighter the complexion, the darker the suit. You *can* wear the lighter shades of blue, but there's a danger of looking washed out if the shade is too light.

SHIRTS. The best colors are blue, red, maroon, burgundy, peach, yellow, and orange.

SHOES. Black leather is the first choice. Stay away from brown.

ACCESSORIES. You should have no problem coordinating ties with the blue suit. Your best choices are maroon, gold, red, burgundy, and blue (lighter or darker than the suit). Stripes or patterns containing these colors will also complement the suit well.

6
DRESSING FOR THE OCCASION

ON THE JOB

This section may well be one of the most important in the book, especially if you have not yet begun your career or are still in high school or college.

Someone once said, "Between five and forty-five seconds after you meet someone, that person has already decided whether he or she likes you or doesn't like you." An exaggeration, perhaps, but it's true that we make snap judgments about people all the time and that these judgments are based largely on the way people dress. That's why it's important to wear appropriate clothes to a job interview, and to see your wardrobe as an integral part of your career plans.

What is appropriate for the job interview? Some say white shirts, some say pastel shirts. But all agree on the dark suit. The idea is to use common sense and not to wear clothes that will draw attention away from *you*.

When in doubt, go conservative. I suggest dark blue and dark gray suits. Solid colors are best. Pin-stripes are acceptable, though they may convey an overdressed impression. I also suggest that your shirt contrast with your suit. White is fail-safe. Pale shades that match your blue or gray suit are acceptable, but the paler the better. Save cufflinks for more formal occasions. Ties should complement suits and their color should be dark. If you want something brighter, try burgundy or a pattern with some white or gold. Your shoes should be black leather or, depending on your complexion and the color of your suit, brown leather. Forget the suedes, patent leathers, and light shades. Never wear brown shoes with a dark blue suit.

The job you land will have a great deal to do with how

you'll want to dress. If you've chosen a career in banking or insurance, for example, you've chosen an area of conservatism. Your dress, your personality, and even your handshake are expected to reflect a person who is trustworthy, level-headed, and in control. That, my man, means that you have to wear a suit, a shirt, and a tie. Something conservative; no frills. The suit should not give any indication of the latest ethnic styles.

Then there are jobs whose rules are less stringent. Record executives, television and advertising people, and even college professors are allowed to wear casual clothes

Don't smoke.

Don't slouch

Don't bring friends or a radio.

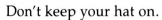

Don't keep your hat on.

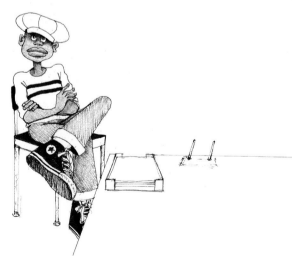

in certain situations, a suit and tie being necessary only for important meetings and business affairs.

According to *Opportunities,* a magazine for minority college graduates, if you are planning to get ahead in the business world, you had better know what the corporate dress code is and conform to it. Corporate dress codes have changed; the gray flannel uniforms have disappeared, and shirts are muted in color. But, however liberalized, a code does exist.

According to Richard V. Clarke, head of his own recruitment agency for college graduates seeking professional employment: "Liberalization of the corporate dress code has been a boon for blacks. The old Brooks Brothers Brahmin uniform has given way to greater variety in lapel size, fitted cuts, and single- and double-vented jackets, all of which are flattering to the black physique." The most successful black executives regard wardrobes as elements in the strategy of getting ahead. Your first step is to acknowledge that the formal regulations governing corporate dress make sense. There is a logic behind them. They're expected; they show respect for the company and for the job.

I'm sure you've heard the saying "You are what you eat." Well, in this case, "You are what you wear." Your clothes send signals to others. It's up to you to make those signals negative or positive images of yourself. The law says that we cannot appear in public naked. We must wear clothes. Therefore, do not take to heart rules that govern corporate dress. Look at it this way: If you want to continue to wear expensive designer clothes and lots of jewelry on your own time, you had better pay attention to those rules or be willing to find another gig.

During my interview session with Richard V. Clarke, he related a story to me that explains the situation in a nutshell. A company's top brass was assembled to hear a presentation on financial projections by a mathematical whiz who was the new genius in the company's administrative staff. The president wore a dark blue suit, a pale blue shirt, and a maroon tie. The executive vice-president wore a three-piece gray suit, a white shirt, and a patterned blue tie. The others, all vice-presidents, sported suits in a variety of medium and dark colors, contrasting light shirts, and conservative ties expertly color-coordinated. The mathematical whiz walked in wearing plaid pants, a dark red shirt, and a loosely knotted purple tie. Whipping off his blue seersucker jacket, he deftly arranged his charts on an easel and launched into a brilliant analysis of the company's cash flow. He proudly explained the new system he had devised to raise enough cash internally so that the corporation wouldn't have to pay inflated interest rates on borrowed money.

After fielding a few superficial questions, he flung his jacket over his arm, picked up his charts, and left the room, confident that his brilliant work would be recognized, that the company would save the $12 million he had estimated as the benefits of his plan, and that he himself would be in line for a fast bonus, a big raise, and a promotion that would leap-frog him over the rest of the pack.

Instead, he was back pounding the street, job-hunting. No sooner had he left the conference than the president had turned to the whiz's immediate boss, the financial vice-president, and said, "Pretty sharp dresser you've got there, Jones." The plan was great, the analysis sound, but the only message that got across was idiosyncratic dress. While some may not agree that you are what you wear, it is true that in corporate life at least, *you become what you appear*.

All of this need not cost a lot of money. One of the biggest problems black men have is in trying to outdress their white counterparts: they do it the wrong way. The brothers go out and spend two weeks' pay on a jacket or suit, not knowing how they will get to work the coming week! That's dumb. Take some time and find out where the discount stores are in your city, or take advantage of sales. If you live in one of the big cities, discount stores are available where you can purchase designer clothes for half the price you would pay in leading clothing stores. There are also discount stores in major cities where you can buy dress shirts, shoes, and pants at good prices. But you have to take some time and find them.

Another way to cut down on expenses for your clothes is through the use of accessories. If your wallet can't take it, instead of trying to have a lot of suits, concentrate on accessories. Several colors of shirts are acceptable in the office. Ties are available in an assortment of stripes, prints, and various hues. So if you can't kill them with suits, accessorize them to the max.

By this time you are probably asking yourself, How is one to know what dress code is in effect? I suggest the following: Observe! You can learn what is going on simply by observation. But don't look at your managers. Observe how your boss dresses and emulate him—within reason, of course. Always dress up to the next step on your career ladder. The style is pretty simple to grasp: dark suits (stay away from black), white or light shirts (pale blue, tans, faded yellow), ties that match or complement the rest of the outfit, and dark leather shoes.

Again, coordination is important. While general conformity to the standard of dress is important, you have to take into account the dress attitudes of your immediate superiors. After all, they are the ones who will recommend or promote you to the next level. Remember, your clothes send signals to others. They can antagonize people or make a good impression. Your dress can suggest honesty, reliability, or other attributes. Mr. Clarke says, "It's not a matter of style over substance, but of style allied to substance to create the image you want to project—the image that will help you in your career." So look at your wardrobe and decide what kind of statement you want to make—the kind of statement that will put you on the road to the executive suite.

AT THE BEACH

Black men have been getting more and more into swimming at the beach and at local swimming pools. They've discovered that swimming is an excellent form of exercise that helps with losing weight and keeping the body trim.

Mike Fields

A favorite pastime at the beach has always been girl watching. But somewhere along the line black men discovered that they were also being watched.

On the whole, beachwear is crazy among black men. They swim in anything from cut-off jeans to running shorts to sweat pants to underwear. It all depends on how much body one wants to show.

Here's a rundown on the more traditional swimsuit styles.

The bikini is the briefest swimsuit on the market. It's about two inches wide at the sides and drops to anywhere from the top of the pubic hair to the crotch. Since the bikini is too small to accommodate a supporter and has no built-in support, it's hard to be generously endowed and feel safe in this suit.

Mike Fields

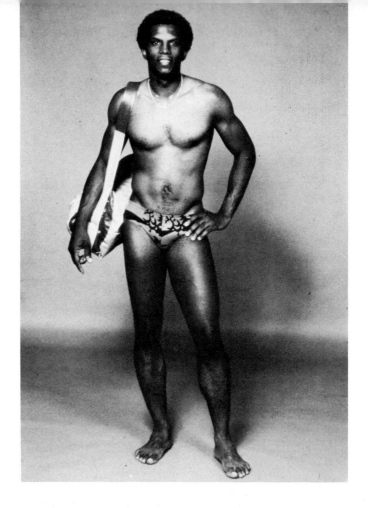

The brief, similar to the nylon underwear that a large majority of black men wear, requires no supporter because it has a same-size or smaller inner lining that provides support. Brief swimwear can have a full, medium, or brief cut, which will affect how wide the suit is cut at the sides.

The boxer swimsuit has gone through many changes. Although the waist is still elastic or has a drawstring, the legs are more tapered and the bagginess is gone. Most boxers have a sheer inner nylon brief for support.

Here are some suggestions for choosing a swimsuit style that best complements your body type:

Mike Fields

Mike Fields

Mike Fields

Mike Fields

The stocky male. Use boxer (or gym-style) trunks. Stay away from the bikini and other brief styles.

The tall, thin male. The standard brief works well with your body type. Don't wear bikini styles or boxer trunks; your legs are too thin for boxers, and the bikini will make you look even thinner.

The Y-shaped male. With your wide top and slim bottom, you should wear boxer trunks. Try to select something with legs that aren't too wide or too tight. You want to balance the overall look as much as possible. Stay away from bikinis or any styles that hug the legs.

The pear-shaped male. You don't want to make your bottom appear any larger, so stick with the tapered boxer swimwear. Avoid bikini styles.

The rotund male. Solid boxer trunks work best. Choose dark solid colors and avoid prints.

ON THE TOWN

The rules of formal wear are very clear-cut. Individuality must be achieved through accessories, because otherwise there's little room for choice. With accessories your look can scale the heights of elegance or make you the preening peacock. Just how brightly you care to glow is totally up to you.

The real staple of formal evening wear is the tuxedo, also commonly referred to as the dinner jacket. The garment got its name from the affluent Tuxedo Park, New York, where it made its first appearance in 1886. The tuxedo, and nothing else, is what's meant by "black tie." If you are someone who enjoys living well and whose career is on the move, you should give a lot of thought to adding a tuxedo to your wardrobe.

Because no updating of a tuxedo is necessary for five or six years, you can think of it as an investment. As with any other suit, quality and fit are all-important. Choose a suit of an essentially conservative cut (single-breasted is always a safer bet than double-breasted) and it will never go out of fashion. Likewise, a notched lapel, rather than a peaked one, will never date you.

If you wear a single-breasted tux, wear a cummerbund or dinner vest in the same fabric and color as the tie. The double-breasted version takes care of the midsection, so you don't need the cummerbund. You *will* need a black bow tie in a fabric that matches your lapel facing.

Since a tuxedo is a suit, your pants should match your jacket. The pants should have a stripe down the side that matches your lapel facing. However, during warm months, when white linen dinner jackets are worn, the pants don't match the jacket at all.

The problem with formal affairs is knowing what to wear when. Just as Fifth Avenue divides the East Side from the West Side in New York City, six P.M. is the line of demarcation between daytime and evening formal occasions. Other factors that must be considered, along with the time of day, are the season, the event, and the role one is playing in it.

If you do not have a tux, you can always rent one for an occasion. If you do, be sure to have a fitting so that you will not be surprised when you get it home. Not having a tux or not being able to rent one need not keep you at home. A navy blue suit will not make you look too much out of place. But don't wear your favorite sports jacket just because your friends say you look damn good in it. Use your own judgment about the situation. If you do check out an affair without a tux, wear your best white shirt and polish your shoes.

7
A Fashion Show

Sporting Hours

Mike Fields

Mike Fields

Leisure Hours

Mike Fields

Business Hours

Charles Stewart

Winter Hours

After Hours

THE AUTHOR would welcome any comments or questions you may have regarding *Getting It Together*. Please direct mail to:

Mike Fields
c/o Dodd, Mead & Company, Inc.
79 Madison Avenue
New York, New York 10016

Index